Copyright© 2016 by Shegitu Kebede. All rights reserved. No part of this book may be used or reproduced in any manner with out prior written permission from the author, except in the case of brief quotations embodied in critical articles and reviews.

Published by Shegitu Kebede, Minnesota, USA

Printed by Gleason Printing, St. Louis Park, Minnesota, USA

ISBN: 978-0-692-66698-2

"...Where the body of the people, or any single man, is deprived of their right, or is under the exercise of a power without right, and have no appeal on earth, then they have a liberty to appeal to heaven, whenever they judge the cause of sufficient moment."

- John Locke, "Second Treatise of Government," 1689-90

Appeal to Heaven
…for a great Nation

Shegitu Kebede

Dedication

To my husband David, without him my dream of making this book a reality would not be possible. And, to my dear children, Menase, Asnat, Jarrett and Philip, my life has been blessed tremendously simply because I have you!

Tribute

I would like to tribute this book to my beloved Mother and true friend, Ann Rock. Ann's life was committed to love and serve people unconditionally. We miss you and look forward to seeing you someday in heaven.

References

All Bible scripture in this book was taken from the King James Version (KJV), which is in public domain. This version was first published in 1611 in what is referred to as Early Modern English. This English text is quite different from what is commonly used today and can prove to be challenging to read in some verses and rather beautiful in others. If necessary, please convert the KJV scriptures in this book to your preferred version for clarity and understanding.

James Madison's Annual Message to Congress, December 5, 1810 : *http://founders.archives.gov*

Theodore Roosevelt's quote in Chapter 3 is from his book, *FEAR GOD and Take Your Own Part*, 1916.

Franklin Roosevelt's address to the crowd in Madison Square Garden, October 28, 1940: *www.presidency.ucsb.edu/ws/?pid=15885*

George Washington's Farewell Address, September 17, 1796: *www.loc.gov/rr/program/bib/ourdocs/farewell.html*

John Hancock's on the anniversary of the Boston Massacre, March 5, 1774: *www.john-hancock-heritage.com/boston-massacre-oration/*

Abraham Lincoln's Lyceum Address, January 27, 1838: *www.abrahamlincolnonline. org/lincoln/speeches/lyceum.htm*

Franklin Roosevelt's radio address, May 27, 1941: *http://docs.fdrlibrary.marist.edu/052741. html*

George Washington's Inaugural Address, April 30, 1789: *www.archives.gov/exhibits/american_ originals/inaugtxt.html*

Ronald Reagan's A Time for Choosing speech, October 27, 1964: *https://reaganlibrary.archives. gov/archives/reference/timechoosing.html*

Patrick Henry's speech is a recollection of memories and accounts collected by William Wirt: *www.history.org/almanack/life/politics/ giveme.cfm*

A transcript of the Declaration of Independence: *www.archives.gov/exhibits/charters/ declaration_transcript.html*

The author of this book has no affiliation with websites or other organizations listed in this book and claim no liability or responsibility for their contents.

x

Contents

Forward	1
Introduction	3
Chapter One: America The Beautiful	28
Chapter Two: Downward Spiral	34
Chapter Three: Be Fruitful	46
Chapter Four: In the Hands of God	54
Chapter Five: Foundation	64
Chapter Six: Religious Indignation	78
Chapter Seven: Misrepresented	92
Chapter Eight: Not My Choice	102
Appendix	112
Acknowledgments	133

Foreword

Appeal to Heaven is filled with a powerful message and passionate viewpoint held by a brave woman named Shegitu Kebede. Her position is bold and countercultural to the America we live in today, yet firmly based in biblical truth. Shegitu's perspective is real and raw, filled with unique insight. Her petition to America is also heartfelt and genuine. As an American immigrant, she sees our country through the eyes of a refugee who has survived horrific personal and political tribulation in her native country of Ethiopia and along the tumultuous journey that brought her to call the United States home over twenty-five years ago.

She loves America and has immense gratitude for her citizenship in this great nation, further validating the importance of the message she has for us in this book.

I have known Shegitu for nearly a decade and continue to be amazed by the impact that she is making in both our local and global communities. She exemplifies the courage and bravery that many admire but few possess. Shegitu leads by example as an authentic leader; her life story and purpose to make a difference has inspired and opened up the eyes of many people previously ignorant to the refugee crisis in this world. I have seen first-hand the influence she has had on some of my college students who have either heard her tell her story or partnered with her organization, Women at the Well International, through a semester-long service learning project assignment. Shegitu is making a difference in our world and this book is one step further towards that goal.

It is my hope that all who read Appeal to Heaven will understand Shegitu's motivation and passion, that her perspective is shaped deeply by her life experience as an orphaned child in a war torn country who escaped and came to the United States as a refugee immigrant full of hope for freedom and a brighter future for herself and her children. She survived what many of us can't even imagine enduring and she desperately wants America to be spared such hardship. As a mother and college professor, I also have high hopes for our country and the next generation of leaders rising up.

What will America be like for them in the coming years? What can we do now to secure their future and ensure that the country we have grown up in will continue to offer the same protection and freedom? Shegitu's message is one of hope, caution, and a heart for our country and the generations to come.

Erica W. Diehn, Ph.D.
October 2015

Introduction

About thirteen years ago I was left alone to raise my children as a single mom. I had to make the hard choice of going to the welfare office for help or do any work I can find as long as it was lawfully and morally acceptable.

As a single mom and a citizen of this country I had the right to ask for a handout but what was important to me was to role model to my children what a Christian mother should be, not just words alone but also my actions. I came from Ethiopia, a socialist country, and I was not only poor but also an orphan. The socialist system didn't allow anyone to dream big or to become someone honorable, yet we were always wishing for some candy of success but nothing of the sort was a reality in a socialist country. Everything was controlled and regulated by the government. It doesn't matter if you have money, you can't buy what you want even though you could afford it. For those who owned cars, gasoline was rationed so you had to take turns to drive the car.

Despite my challenges, I had the desire and determination to give my children a better life then I had. I couldn't imagine what affects the chaos and trauma of my divorce had on my young children. To reverse that effect and to avoid the cycle of broken family and poverty I needed a different mindset. To have any chance of success on what I was dreaming for my kids I needed to put the biggest distance between them and poverty. The last thing I wanted to do was to be on government assistance. Even though I did not have money there are things I considered a blessing. So I put my best foot forward, which was, I had been granted and blessed by God with good health and capable mind. I worked many hours tirelessly day and night to make sure my kids could stay in our own home, sleep in their own beds, stay in our neighborhood and go to same school they were familiar with. That was so important to me to stabilize their lives and provide a routine structure to impact their future positively.

It was my determination to raise my kids without hearing the words "we can't afford it." So they had the latest electronic gadgets necessary to improve their future, and automobiles when they turned sixteen. Why? Because I wanted them to know that no matter what your circumstance in life is, you're in a country where it is possible to have whatever you want if you work hard for it.

My goal and driving point was even with someone like their mother, who is a new first generation immigrant, accent and all, can work hard to fulfill her dreams, then how much easier should it be for them. That was my unspoken message and was so important for me to show them.

If any possibility existed, I made a point every single day to let them know it is possible in this land we call United States of America. I also let them know that God has given us the opportunity in this country not just to take up space and resources but also to make something of our lives and to better humanity.

Today, it is so hard for me to understand why people are trying to abolish the privilege we have in this country and are buying into an ideology of nonsense. We are raising the next generation on a false promise, drawing a picture in society's mind that being American is bad so we must remove our values to embrace someone else's. At the same time the rest of the world is trying to look like America or come to America. The only people who are having a hard time being American are those who are in America! One other thing that puzzles me is those who had been oppressed, discriminated against and driven out of their country, come to America to get their freedom and all the sudden it seems like they get the notion to attack the very country that gave them this platform. Instead of being grateful for the life and liberty America has to offer they want to turn it back into a system they left behind.

This unique system we received is ours to preserve for future generations and future immigrants. We have to revive the attitude of "if you want something then you need to work for it" instead of "we give you free." We need to show that it takes work to create a better life. From my own personal experience as an orphan and refugee, if someone had given me something, it was never what my heart desired but only what I needed. Why limit yourself to survival when you can thrive and experience life to the fullest.

Those who support this "get for free" notion need to understand and realize that those politicians who are promising us free this or that's are doing so just to get elected. Where are the free things coming from, out of thin air? We need to ask these very questions and examine every idea. We can't just buy into ideas if we discount common sense, we might be destroying our future.

For the last fifteen years or so I have been blessed to hear many scholars and experts speak on a variety of subjects. Some of the subjects include what I'm talking about in this book. I'm the kind of person that doesn't like to see people taken advantage of and I don't like to just sit back when wrong things prevail. I heard this argument from both sides of what the original intention of our Founders was and how we see ourselves now in the twenty-first century.

As a mother and grandmother it alarms and concerns me about the direction our country has taken. I decided to dig deep to learn more about how this country came to be. What is my roll as an American? What will my children and their children's future look like if I let this misleading movement continue? I want to make sure everyone is given an opportunity to hear from those of us who had the experience of living under a different ideology.

Our colleges and universities who fought for freedom of expression and open ideas over the past years are today making them pools of one-sided liberal ideology - that is not freedom. Despite these challenges, those of us who still believe in the American Dream and the Founding values need to make it our mission to bring the truth to everyone.

For our next generation, we need to model what we received from the previous generation. We need to show them that if you want something, work for it, instead of "we will give it to you for free." It's our responsibility to model the way so they can work and create something that will better their life and the generation after them that is the American way!

We need to hear what is like to live in a country counter to our ideology. The grass always looks greener on the other side, but I suggest we need to look closely to get the full story before we move to the other side. Although it seems exciting at first to steer our country in a new direction, I caution us to think before jumping off a new wagon.

I would like to point out that American ideology is proven. It has been working for centuries and is why you do not find anyone living in this country going elsewhere to find a better life. Yet people from all over the world are coming to this country to achieve their dreams because it was impossible to do so where they were from.

I find that American culture gets bored quickly. Do not let us waste our energy fixing a foundation that is not broken. Instead, let us fix the crack in our system and build on the original foundation for a better tomorrow. It is necessary to do our homework and find the truth for ourselves and to make a sound decision individually and collectively before we destroy this one of kind privileged way of living.

Let us make it our duty to find out why previous leaders and the Founding Fathers set things in place the way they did. Why was there a biblical basis for their decisions on the issue of moral |values? What influenced their thinking? How did they come to a conclusion to write the Declaration of Independence? And what was the purpose behind it? Was their culture a factor? Do we have credible evidence that their faith played a role? Or was it their upbringing or personal preference that played the influencing role? What I have come to understand is that the Founding Fathers held certain principles of faith. Those for, and those opposed to the founders had produced a commendable amount of information and both could be right to a certain extent.

I want to be clear, I'm not writing this book to prove or disprove anyone. I even believe that it wasn't the intent of our Founding Fathers to force their values upon individuals or to not have room for anything else. That was not the case at all. Rather you will find their value of faith was personal and thus, their guiding light. It is very crucial to understand why collectively the Founding Fathers come in agreement to build this nation on Christian values even though as we can see from the evidence that not all of them were Christians. Their reason was clearly Christian, but was not intimidated by other religions and always welcomed all religion. Christian nations have always co-existed side by side with other religions. One example is Ethiopia, which historically it is believed to be the oldest Christian nation. It began when Phillip explained the gospel of Jesus to an Ethiopian eunuch, the treasurer under the Candace queen of the Ethiopians. This encounter took place as the Ethiopian was returning home from Jerusalem (see the Book of Acts 8: 26-39).

Ethiopia had adopted and lived by the Christian value for many centuries following this encounter and has co-existed with Judaism, Islam and many other religions. In contrary to this, where Christianity is not tolerated usually freedoms of other religions are suppressed as well, save the dominant one. In conclusion, when Christianity has been freely welcomed in nations other religions are welcome also. This fact has been proven throughout history.

"Of all the dispositions and habits which lead to political prosperity, religion and morality are indispensable supports. In vain would that man claim the tribute of patriotism, who should labor to subvert these great pillars of human happiness, these firmest props of the duties of men and citizens.

The mere politician, equally with the pious man, ought to respect and to cherish them. A volume could not trace all their connections with private and public felicity. Let it simply be asked: Where is the security for property, for reputation, for life, if the sense of religious obligation desert the oaths which are the instru ments of investigation in courts of justice? And let us with caution indulge the supposition that morality can be maintained without religion.

Whatever may be conceded to the influence of refined education on minds of peculiar structure, reason and experience both forbid us to expect that national morality can prevail in exclusion of religious principle."

- George Washington, excerpt from Farewell Address to the People of the United States, 1796

When our Founding Fathers build our country on biblical principles they were looking out for our society from every angle, not just from religious perspectives. I also point out that some of the Fathers may not have been believers in the narrowest sense of the term, yet in the larger sense that influences culture, their thinking was thoroughly Christian. They may not be "Christian" in today's sense but they were God-fearing men and deeply influenced by a biblical view of man and government. They understood that the fear of God, moral leadership, and a righteous community of people were necessary for their great experiment to succeed.

They knew if they sought the establishment of a just society, Christianity was the only religion that could accommodate that and have room for everyone else's religion. I believe the Founders view and one reason for choosing biblical values, wasn't to convert the masses to Christianity, but, was knowing the biblical way of Christianity is the only one that made room for all without discrimination.

Even though our society today is fixed upon the idea of ridding itself of God and Christianity I think it's in our best interest to dig deeper and try to understand why our Founding Fathers chose Christian values to build their new nation. Once we clearly see their intent it's easy to conclude that it has nothing to do with converting or forcing anyone to Christianity, but it's all about creating a healthy and well-functioning society. When I think about the concept of "Separation of Church and State" I think there's a serious misunderstanding of the Founders intent. When this concept was conceived our Founding Fathers remembered the system they left behind and it was evident to them that the Church sided with the government, or more so, that the government controlled the church. The church, as an extension of the government, was used to force people to compliance in name of God because at the time the common person didn't have ready access to a Bible. There was a twisting of the Word by so-called "church leaders" even to the point of threatening one's salvation in order to maintain control over the population.

My theory is that the concept of "Separation of Church and State" was put in place so that this corrupt relationship between Kings and Queens and the church would not be imposed on this new country and people. It was never the intent to remove Christian values from our government and public squares. When I consider the moral direction of our society over the last fifty years I can clearly see a steady departure from Christian values. The family structure has been broken and the resulting ripple effect is driving the divorce rate higher. The spin-off effect this has is a lack of affirmed discipline and guidance at home.

A large percent of our children are suffering from depression and the suicide rate among teenagers and young adults is at all-time high. Addiction, chemical dependency and other destructive behavior among the youth continue to rise. Rebellion against authority figures is growing rapidly and race relations have eroded severely in the last several years. Some inner city teachers are afraid for their life from the very students they are supposed to educate. Most of our media, which has been our trusted source news and information, have become one-sided or agenda driven to the point of deception. It doesn't bother us anymore, and in fact, has become a normal way of life to see children insult parents and elders and youth disrespect adults. When did we allow this to become acceptable in our culture? How will our children differentiate between right and wrong? Where are the limits?

When it comes to broken families, instead of parents becoming role models that provide structure and values for their family, the focus is to fill the void and guilt of separation or divorce. Parents are competing for the children's love and approval. But in the process of this treadmill the children lack a firm foundation and the structure they need. We are raising a shallow generation with an entitlement mentality. Research has shown that one of the top seven reasons why marriages end in divorce is a lack of religious affiliation. When you look at all this chaos in our society you can trace it back to ungodliness, and humanity is crying out to anyone that can hear, "I can't handle all this by myself." We have thrown money and expert advice on these issues but nothing is improving, as a matter of fact, it's getting worst.

This nation is losing respect as a global leader because of the way we conduct ourselves. I'm not seeing the benefits of removing God by steering away from the principles that our founders put in place. It is safe to say from these facts that form our understanding of thisrelationship between religion and government, that it has been structured this way for a reason. Dismantling it may result in the dismantling of the very way of life, we enjoy here in these United States.

As a first generation American I have my own perspective and it is drawn from my experiences. I'm inviting you to peek through the windows of my past and present with the hope that after you read my story and looking through the evidence of world history, you will make your own decision.

I lost my closest family members and never had the opportunity to witness a funeral or grieve properly for any of them. I was five when we lost our mom and dad. And later I would lose my two brothers. After losing our parents, my brothers and I ended up in orphanage. At that time I had one older brother and two younger brothers. I believe I was about eleven or twelve years of age when the Socialist soldiers picked my oldest brother and forced him to be a child soldier. That was the last time we saw him.

Being an orphan we didn't have anyone to protect us. My younger siblings and I, along with other orphan kids, were left on our own to figure out this big world by ourselves. I set out to do that. At 16 years of age I was the only grown up left in my family so it was my responsibility to find a way to protect my two younger brothers.

I got married thinking I might be able to provide a safe home for my brothers. A few months in, I learned and realized life sometimes never goes as you planned. I was left with no other choice but to run to save my, and my unborn child's life. I arrived at a refugee camp and later to the United States just to learn the bad news that I had lost yet one more brother. You can imagine my pain, my regret, and the guilt I felt for leaving them behind even though there was nothing I could do. I knew that I was not in any shape to protect them nor had the ability to. But that didn't stop me from feeling guilty and beating myself up for surviving.

Running away for the Socialist government was illegal and anyone who got caught would be killed right on the spot. My journey was a very nerve-racking experience; I was walking at night to avoid being caught by the Socialist soldiers. If you got caught, they would do the unthinkable to you before killing you. I crossed the border safely into Kenya, the neighboring country, but was thrown into jail where I was not able to communicate and explain my situation since they did not speak my language and I did not speak theirs. Even though it was frustrating, I had no choice but to be at their mercy and patiently hope for a positive outcome. I was there for four weeks not knowing what was going on.

Finally, I was granted permission to go to the refugee camp. After that terrifying experience I made it to the refugee camp and later to the United States.

My journey did not start with the luxury of packing bags with necessary things for my trip. Not a map, nor a plan to do things on way, or a chance to pencil in some sightseeing. This journey was running for dear life with only the clothes on my back. Only by common knowledge of the direction of my destination, without any navigational system and without knowing how long it would take to if get there (if I ever did), without a meal or accommodation plan, did I embark on my journey. It was a journey of faith. I do not have the proper words to describe how scared I was walking in that pitch-dark night, while hearing wild animals in the distance. The only thing I could do to calm my nerves was to talk to myself.

My heart was beating fast, my hands were sweating, my knees were about give in, I was terrified! But I continued walking. Many times I thought to myself, "How can God exist?" And if He still existed, "How could he allow a Seventeen-year-old child to be so terrified and alone like this?"

In many occasions I honestly felt that nobody understood or cared about what happen to orphans and refugees like me. There were also times I almost gave up and did not care what happened to me anymore. The facts were that as soon as I overcame one misery, the next one was just around the corner. At times it felt like I had lost grip on reality. Since I was five I was left alone to figure life out by myself, especially after my older brother disappeared.

The unfairness and injustice I had felt and witnessed caused anger and rage inside me but there was no way to justify it. I did not find anyone who truly cared or understood what was hurting me. I was crying out of my fear and pain, in my deepest sorrow, but no one was there to comfort me.

At times, I felt there must be something wrong with me or that I had to be a bad person to have experienced all this pain. In my culture, it has been believed that it's the fault of the children, who lose their parents at a young age, as if they were bad luck to their parents. After hearing this many times, I grew and took it to heart - blaming myself for the death of my parents. I came to the realization that the environment and cultures we grow up in have a lot of influence in our lives. I was brought up in the church. One of the turn-offs towards the church, for me as a child, was the view of God by so called "church leaders." They displayed unbiblical behavior when I was growing up. They treated me rudely, which was something I had witnessed many times before. That sent me heading in different direction. At a young age, I made up my mind that I would have nothing to do with religion or God.

I remember hearing when my younger brother had been shot in the war. The Socialist government didn't care for wounded soldiers so he was sent home. When my brother arrived home, the church did not give him the medical care he needed. At that time the missionaries in my orphanage had been sent back to their home countries and although their clinics and schools had been left in the custody of those who used to work with the missionaries, they did not find it necessary to care for my brother because he was an orphan.

Instead they threw him out into the street and he died soon after. They even went as far as refusing to bury him in the church cemetery because he was not a good enough Christian for them. I had witnessed many injustices since I was young, but this event became a turning point. It brought me to the conclsion that I would never have anything to do with God or anyone associated with Him.

I'm very certain that if it weren't for the Christians I had encountered in Nairobi, Kenya, I would have missed the greatest opportunity of my life. They showed me a completely different portrait of what a Christian is with their life and deeds. That is why it's so crucial to not make decisions based only on at-hand circumstances. When I began to think with a clear and calm mind I came to understand that although the cross is the symbol for Christianity, the day Jesus hung on the cross there were

18

actually three crosses. Two of them symbolize how we have been reconciled to God - the third was the imitator.

"The thief cometh not, but for to steal, and to kill, and to destroy: I am come that they might have life, and that they might have it more abundantly."

-John 10:10

This imitator did not get his start on the cross, his intentions were to steal, kill and destroy lives since the very beginning - starting with the first family in Garden of Eden. There are moments in our life that shift our thinking and perspective.

For me it was this verse in Genesis 3:8-9. If we look at the first family's turning point, they did not understand who they were, and they bought into a lie. They were deceived the moment they believed in getting a new identity, not realizing that in the process they lost who they were. Scripture shows us that God is asking them a sort of, "Where are you with your new identity?" He's saying to them, "How's it working for you?" As we can see from the story this "new identity" did not give them what they were expecting, but instead they found themselves in a state of shame, wanting to hide from God.

"8 And they heard the voice of the Lord God walking in the garden in the cool of the day: and Adam and his wife hid themselves from the presence of the Lord God amongst the trees of the garden.
9 And the Lord God called unto Adam, and said unto him, Where art thou?"

- Genesis 3:8-9

God, in His mercy, did not leave them in shame but He made a way for them to come to terms. All along there was no need to go through the loops of a new identity, rather just come back to the original intent. As a nation and as individuals we might be in the same scenario. Now it's our turn, let us do some soul-searching and come back to our true identity.

Life can be messy at times. We are human and we always tend to make mistakes, but God knows that. He lets us come to Him just the way we are- with all the mess. As long as we acknowledge our brokenness and cry out to God for help with a sincere heart, He is more than willing to heal our land and to restore us again. I have been there myself. I've experienced the pain of being scared, helpless and bruised yet when I cried out to Him, He heard me! He did not look away like people do, He does not consult our background, and He does not care what we've done in the past or what we've failed to do. The good news about God's amazing character is that He is a loving God! The minute we say sorry and turn away from our old ways, it is completely forgotten.

"³⁴ Then Peter opened his mouth, and said, Of a truth I perceive that God is no respecter of persons:
³⁵ But in every nation he that feareth him, and worketh righteousness, is accepted with him."
- Acts 10: 34-35

As a reminder it doesn't matter to God what sin consumed us in the past. He is able to take anyone out of that situation as long as we are willing to take the responsibility to live in the freedom He continuously offers us. God's love, forgiveness and kindness are immeasurable. We just need to be willing to leave behind our past and move in a new direction. The pain is real regardless of what culture or circumstances say so as long as we are alive this is the reality we face. But also, I come to the realization that I have the choice not to be bitter, or to be held hostage by pain and hate.

Those choices are in my hand and it led me to a crossroads in life. I made up my mind to not live in the past because life is to precious and to short to spend it looking back. Bitterness and self-pity is not for me. Knowing that the Master Healer has touched me, it was now up to me to live a healthy life. I realized pain itself could be a gift, a gift that God can use to teach me. I can learn from the pain and help others through it. Pain can also bring out what's in us. Every encounter we have in life can be a lesson and opportunity to better our self and those around us. I need to acknowledge that God did not cause any of my pain. It was the circumstances and ideology of the people around me, and my own bad choices. I realized bitterness and self-pity can make my life and the lives of those around me miserable. I have been given a different perspective in life, so I make choices now with sound judgment.

My survival is attributed to the unwavering truth of the Word of God. I read it, believed it, lived it, stood on it and knew it had the power to change me - and it continues to change me every day. I should point out I'm not strong or wise or special or a "holy person;" I'm an average person like everybody else. I'm sharing my story because story telling is the one thing that connects us all and I believe we can be one another's strength. We are visible when linked with one another. My hope is we learn and become inspired by one another's story so as to prevent us from making the same mistakes in the future.

It is up to all of us to take the necessary steps to secure our liberty - a liberty that is very rare.

"Only a life lived for others is a life worthwhile."
- Albert Einstein

That is why I felt compelled to tell this worthwhile story of America and how the title "Appeal to Heaven" came about. I found it my necessary duty as a citizen of this great land to tell the true story of our nation and how I see that it is so important to preserve. The story of this land is a story of us all, how we came to be called "Americans." We are a one-of-a-kind and blessed people and this is the only place on earth that such a diverse body of people live and prosper peacefully. I strongly believe that it is "our story" that needs to be told. When we don't know who we are and where we come from, we don't appreciate who we are and where we are going. We did not get here out of nothing. Someone had to pay the price for us to enjoy this one-of-a-kind life.

"Give Me Liberty Or Give Me Death!"
-Patrick Henry

How many of you know the story of Patrick Henry? How about George Washington, John Adams, Thomas Jefferson, Abraham Lincoln and Ronald Reagan, just to name a few? Where did the phrase "Give Me Liberty Or Give Me Death!" come from? What does that phrase mean to you? The phrase comes from a speech by Patrick Henry in 1775 and is included at the end of this book. The attitude of our Founding Fathers and of previous generations was selflessness.

It is my desire to help my fellow Americans realize this unique opportunity and the responsibility we have been entrusted with to preserve this idea, and pass it on to the next generation in an even better shape than we have received it.

"Beyond those monuments to heroism is the Potomac River, and on the far shore the sloping hills of Arlington National Cemetery with its row on row of simple white markers bearing crosses

or Stars of David Under one such marker lies a young man--Martin Treptow--who left his job in a small town barber shop in 1917 to go to France with the famed Rainbow Division. There, on the western front, he was killed trying to carry a message between battalions under heavy artillery fire.

We are told that on his body was found a diary. On the flyleaf under the heading, "My Pledge," he had written these words: "America must win this war. Therefore, I will work, I will save, I will sacrifice, I will endure, I will fight cheerfully and do my utmost, as if the issue of the whole struggle depended on me alone."

- Ronald Reagan First Inaugural address,
Tuesday, January 20, 1981

As we read young Martin Treptow short but heroic story and hear of his devotion to this country and sacrifice he makes for all of us, I realize the freedom I have in this country did not come free, someone paid that price with his or her life. Now it's our turn, how do we respond? The rest of the world is looking from the outside at the United States of America and they know and acknowledge that this nation is set apart. This unique lifestyle and freedom for every man and woman to choose their own destiny, to work and produce, is only given in the United States of America. That's what sets us apart from the rest of the world.

Today we are shying away from that truth with rushing speed. Our Founding Fathers built this beautiful nation for you and I to enjoy. We are to preserve this one-of-a-kind privilege that had been passed on to us and are obligated to pass it onto our children. The Founders principle was based on fearing God.

"It cannot be emphasized too strongly or to often that this great Nation was founded not by religionists, but by Christians; not on religion, but on the Gospel of Jesus Christ. For that reason alone, people of other faiths have been afforded freedom of worship here."
- Patrick Henry, 1776

"It is impossible to rightly govern a nation without God and the Bible."
- George Washington

"Our Constitution was made only for a moral and religious people. It is wholly inadequate to the government of any other."
- John Adams

"The highest glory of the American Revolution was this: it connected in one indissoluble bond the principles of civil government with the principles of Christianity."
- John Quincy Adams

"The United States of America was no longer-Colonies. They were an independent nation of Christians."
- John Quincy Adams

Chapter One
America The Beautiful

I arrived in the United States in the winter season of the late 1980s. Once the cold winter season was over, I noticed how beautiful this land was, and how quickly the earth forgave its lifelessness. Everything reclaims its color and shows off the lush green. The grass becomes lavish green, the leaves on the trees sprout with such splendor. Everything was amazingly gorgeous!

That is not the only thing I have noticed about this wonderful country. The people are also beautiful inside and out. It is these very people that make the fabric of this great land. The people in this great nation take pride in hard work, making a name for themselves and making a difference in this land and in the world.

When I was still brand new to this country, I saw how people come together to help their neighbors. For instance, if there is a tornado or any kind of natural disaster in their own state or elsewhere in the country, people often came together to support each other. I fell in love with the spirit of volunteerism that I saw being valued by the majority of Americans. The people in this land do these kinds of things as if they are obligated. Americans seem to believe that helping others is a sacred obligation. It is a lifestyle. That was great to witness. Again and again I have noticed how ordinary people came together to help one another. This kindness and spirit of giving was not reserved only for their own people or those living in their own country, but this kindness was also extended to many nations around the world.

One thing that I have noticed about Americans is that when they help others, they do not wonder if they are liked or loved by the people they are helping, they simply help because they see a need. That was beautiful to witness as well. A few years ago my business partner and I had personally experienced some major setbacks in our business. It was so bad that we were about to close our business, but one of our American friends found out and shared our story with her friends and colleagues as well as strangers via email. Many people did the same and the email snowballed. Their decision to share our story with their network of friends caused a large number of people to contribute toward helping us. As a result of their kindness and generosity our business is still open.

That is what America is all about, and that is what makes America so unique and different from the rest of the world. When I was preparing for my citizenship, I studied American history, the Constitution and the law of this great land. It was then that I learned that those who had experienced tyranny in their home countries crafted this Constitution. They were determined to avoid tyrannical and socialist ideologies in the making of America.

The founders of the United States set out to do something honorable, honest and desirable. They were carving out something new, something noble and unique! The secret to their solid foundation was that the founders who drafted the Declaration of Independence and the Constitution consulted the Holy Bible. They understood that wisdom and knowledge came from the Scriptures.

The founders of America put together something firm to govern their country and their people. That uniqueness has set them apart from the rest of the world. There is no question about it. That is why millions of people around the world desire to be a part of this great nation. America has been an inspiration and role model for the entire world. As an individual who was about to become an American, what I understood is that when I live by the founding principles, I think and behave as an American and not in terms of party affiliation or special interests. That is commendable!

Chapter Two
Downward Spiral

Today, the same people I had fallen in love with, who have been my inspiration, are about to fall. I see them heading in the wrong direction, something I had witnessed in my native country and similarly in many socialist countries. My heart is breaking for us.

I see our nation now being led in a disturbing direction, not discerning fact from fiction. Those who hate this one of kind way of living and freedom are deceiving the people to destroy. It seems that overnight our nation has become rebellious against God and the principles that the founders embraced while forming these United States.

"Whilst it is universally admitted that a well-instructed people alone can be permanently a free people…"

- James Madison in his Annual Message to Congress, Dec 5, 1810

Since this nation has become blind to what is going on, its values and principles are being stripped right before its eyes and the lifestyle people have enjoyed is slipping out of their hands. Among other things, we have come to a place where we are redefining what God had put in place since the creation of mankind, when He decreed that marriage be between man and woman. We are enticing ourselves to hasten our downfall as a society by taking it upon ourselves to change God's establishment of the sanctity of marriage dating back to The Garden of Eden.

Let us look back and see what happened in Germany when Hitler rose to power. In just few years he changed the health care, enforced gun control, nationalized education, and shut down free exercise of religion. Germany lost its conscience and many sat back silently while millions of Jewish people were railroaded to concentration camp and subsequently murdered. We need to reflect on whether or not we see a difference between Nazi Germany and the direction where we are heading? If we continue in this way of ungodliness, I fear that our country may end up in the same condition as Hitler's Germany.

When we consider the case of the refugees who are fleeing for their lives from Middle Eastern and North African countries, they are not running and seeking refuge in Muslim countries or other countries run by what we consider tyrannical dictators. They are going to countries where there is freedom of religion and a free way of living. On the other hand, we in America are heading in the opposite direction. If our nation does not turn back to God, dictatorship, disaster and destruction will become a normal way of living for our nation.

It is important to emphasize that if any destruction is manifested in our nation, it is not God who is causing it, but our own self-destructive behavior. Think of it this way;

"Be not deceived; God is not mocked: for whatsoever a man soweth, that shall he also reap"
-Galatians 6:7

An example of the manifestation of this verse in our society can be clearly seen in the area of the redefinition of marriage as mentioned earlier. We sowed acceptance of the homosexual lifestyle, and we reaped a demand for same-sex marriage. This is open defiance of God's definition of marriage as being between one man and one woman. He put this in place when He created the first man and woman. Only God knows what we will reap from that, but one thing is certain, we are tempting the speedy downfall of our society.

I know at this time and age it is not politically correct or popular to say what I am saying. However, if we discount God's way and base everything solely on other people's opinion or what's acceptable in society, then we would live a life only to please others. That is not freedom and is exactly what the United States Constitution was designed to prevent. We were granted freedom of speech and freedom of religion so that we would not be enslaved by the views and ideals of a few. Never compromise the truth and what is right. If you look at any of the inventors and creators of new products and technologies - from airplanes to cars to computers - many had encountered resistance, some even mockery by society. Yet imagine what modern-day life would be like if all the inventors gave in to the ridicule of skeptics and naysayers.

Do you remember when President Ronald Reagan set out to protect the United States from the Soviet Union, labeled "The Evil Empire"? Millions of Americans were protesting against his actions and even mocking his Strategic Defense Initiative, a space based missile defense system. Imagine if President Reagan would of caved to this pressure and then scaled back his defense plans against the Soviet Union. It's safe to say that communism would have continued to spread and our world would look much different today.

Speaking of Communism, in 1980, at the time President Reagan was defending the United States from the ideology of Communist Soviet Union, it was too late for my family and my country. I was 12 years old and I was living a life of misery. It is crucial to understand my passion and story in order to relate to and comprehend where I am coming from. I was born in Ethiopia in the late 1960's.

My country was in transition from kingdom rule to socialism. Ethiopia had a Christian king and freedom of religion at that time but in the midst of a revolution fell prey to influence by the Soviet Union. In the midst of that chaos, I found myself with my three brothers in the orphanage. We thought that was the hardest part of our lives until we lost our missionary parents, who were the orphan caregivers. This caused us to experience the loss of our parents for the second time. Our missionary parents at the orphanage were forced to leave the country along with their embassy and the embassies of other western nations. This included the United States, who had no association with communism. That is when the real meaning of suffering and misery hit home. My story is narrated in detail in my previous book Visible Strengths, Hidden Scars.

The communist movement that came to my country at that time had no respect for life – this was especially the case for Christians. I see a similarity between what I experienced in the "socialization" of Ethiopia and what is starting to happen in our nation today. Speaking frankly, I fear for our country's future. Sometimes I ask myself, "Why should it bother me so much? Why should I feel this way?" Now I understand my feelings because the fundamental transformation I see in the United States today are reminiscent of the baby steps I seen in the decline of my home country. I've been there and I don't want to experience it again, nor do not want anyone else to experience it either.

I am amazed when I think of America. How the citizens of a nation that has experienced so much freedom could be lured into a trap of deception and fear. I reflect on how far we have strayed from the fundamental truth of freedom. For the nation that never gives in to anything I cannot process how far we have fallen.

During this period in Ethiopia, Christianity was considered intolerable. The newly formed socialist government forced onto the population the notion that Christianity was unnecessary and as a matter of fact, it was communicated that Christians were the cause of all the problems in the world. The goal was to eliminate Christianity and God so that we could all become "justified and equal." It is ironic when they say that, but when you look at world history, wherever Christianity and the value of faith is persecuted, that's where you'l fine people deprived of real freedom.

We were all required to gather in stadiums and on the streets so as to march against God. We were forced to carry banners reading, "There is No God", and "What made Mankind was the work of his own hand", and "Down with Imperialism." The leaders organized many big meetings. They built town halls and stadiums in every city, and forced people to rally and be brainwashed by their communist ideology.

After nearly two decades of living in the United States, I had the opportunity to revisit Ethiopia. Those who said there was "No God" have themselves long disappeared along with their ideology, but God is still on His throne. Here's the great irony in all this. The very meeting halls and stadiums built to gather the unwilling no longer support forced socialist propaganda, but are now being filled with worshipping Christians.

"But as for you, ye thought evil against me; but God meant it unto good, to bring to pass, as it is this day, to save much people alive"

- Genesis 50:20

No nation ever stands against God and continues to prosper for long.

"Why do the heathen rage, and the people imagine a vain thing[?]"

- Psalm 2:1

Let us save ourselves from these vain pursuits. I have survived a great deal of ups and downs in my life. The key to my survival has been the grace of God and the kindness of people who are willing to believe and stand up to do the right thing.

That is why it is so important for me not to worry about being politically correct. Rather, I believe the very reason I survived the misery I encountered in the past was so that I might speak up at this very moment. I believe America is at a very significant crossroads. Whether we believe it or not, this struggle will determine the survival or the destruction of this great nation.

We are facing a cosmic struggle between good and evil, and we need to carefully discern the difference so we know where to stand. We have become a society that believes in subjective morality and personal preference instead of the solid foundational truth found in the Bible.

In the name of freedom and civilization, that subjective morality and personal preference have led to a culture where a sinful lifestyle is accepted as a normal way of life.

"Woe unto them that call evil good, and good evil; that put darkness for light, and light for darkness; that put bitter for sweet, and sweet for bitter"

-Isaiah 5:20

Chapter Three
Be Fruitful

The Almighty God has blessed the works of our hands, and our nation grew strong and wealthy, but those achievements have filled us with pride and become our idols in the process. Our leaders have misused much of that wealth to create a culture of entitlement. As a result, each generation has become more and more dependent on government handouts and less dependent on God and their God-given abilities. We bought into the promise of a quick fix. Instead, we have passive living with little or no expectation, no drive or ambition to work hard. The philosophy of the generation we are producing seems to convey; "Whatever happens will happen." This nonchalant attitude is the complete opposite of the principles on which this country was founded.

The result is the fruit of an ungodly society. The Bible says;

"For even when we were with you, this we commanded you, that if any would not work, neither should he eat"
- 2 Thessalonians 3:10

(See also Timothy 5:8, Proverbs 28:19)

Our ability to work and produce good fruit is the gift from God to men, and what our hands produce is our gift to humanity and God. That was one of the ideas that had been impressed upon me about America, but today I see a different breed of Americans.

"But in addition to fearing God, it is necessary that we should be able and ready to take our own part. The man who cannot take his own part is a nuisance in the community, a source of weakness, an encouragement to wrongdoers and an added burden to the men who wish to do what is right. If he cannot take his own part, then somebody else has to take it for him."

- Theodore Roosevelt, 1916

"We guard against the forces of anti-Christian aggression which may attack us from without, and the forces of ignorance and fear which may corrupt us from within."

- President Franklin Delano Roosevelt, Madison Square Garden, October 28, 1940

Our new way of living and the choices some of us are currently making are no different from what history tells us about other nations that rose and fell. It can all be traced back to ungodliness; there is no doubt about it. The Bible says:

"For the wages of sin is death; but the gift of God is eternal life through Jesus Christ our Lord"

- Romans 6: 23

I believe our nation is dying, but God in His sovereignty will never judge a society without a warning. We see many examples in the Bible. I am also doing my part by warning my nation and my generation.

"Surely the Lord God will do nothing, but he revealeth his secret unto his servants the prophets"

- Amos 3:7

God has been revealing His plan to His servants like Abraham, Noah, Samuel, Jeremiah and many others throughout the centuries. God is Holy and just. He never does anything without giving us a warning, an opportunity to turn back to Him and repent from our wrongdoing. I like to also mention that God is not a dictator. He does not impose Himself on anyone. He wants us to follow Him and worship Him willingly so He has given us a free choice.

"[11] For this commandment which I command thee this day, it is not hidden from thee, neither is it far off.
[12] It is not in heaven, that thou shouldest say, Who shall go up for us to heaven, and bring it unto us, that we may hear it, and do it?
[13] Neither is it beyond the sea, that thou shouldest say, Who shall go over the sea for us, and bring it unto us, that we may hear it, and do it?
[14] But the word is very nigh unto thee, in thy mouth, and in thy heart, that thou mayest do it.
[15] See, I have set before thee this day life and good, and death and evil;
[16] In that I command thee this day to love the Lord thy God, to walk in his ways, and to keep his commandments and his statutes and his judgments, that thou mayest live and multiply: and the Lord thy God shall bless thee in the land whither

thou goest to possess it.

[17] But if thine heart turn away, so that thou wilt not hear, but shalt be drawn away, and worship other gods, and serve them;

[18] I denounce unto you this day, that ye shall surely perish, and that ye shall not prolong your days upon the land, whither thou passest over Jordan to go to possess it.

[19] I call heaven and earth to record this day against you, that I have set before you life and death, blessing and cursing: therefore choose life, that both thou and thy seed may live:

[20] That thou mayest love the Lord thy God, and that thou mayest obey his voice, and that thou mayest cleave unto him: for he is thy life, and the length of thy days: that thou mayest dwell in the land which the Lord sware unto thy fathers, to Abraham, to Isaac, and to Jacob, to give them"

-Deuteronomy 30:11-20

Chapter Four
In the Hands of God

Some may say if God were merciful and good why would He destroy us? Think of it this way: Imagine a home security system company. A person needs to be working with or have good relationships with that company in order to be protected by them. Just because they are in the home security business does not mean that every homeowner is under their protection.

"6 If we say that we have fellowship with him, and walk in darkness, we lie, and do not the truth:
7 But if we walk in the light, as he is in the light, we have fellowship one with another, and the blood of Jesus Christ his Son cleanseth us from all sin.
8 If we say that we have no sin, we deceive ourselves, and the truth is not in us.
9 If we confess our sins, he is faithful and just to forgive us our sins, and to cleanse us from all unrighteousness.
10 If we say that we have not sinned, we make him a liar, and his word is not in us"

- John 1:6-10

There are terms and conditions, and the company only protects those who have a contracts with them. Essentially the same principle applies to our relationship with God. For more than two centuries our nation was protected and favored by God. Now, our nation has been warned time and time again about its rebellious ways. So now, let us make a sound decision to save ourselves. It seems like we let go of God for so long and many wrong decisions have been made on our behalves and we have turned a blind eye because of fear or apathy. My question today for any American is, "Do you know that you are going through a cultural war?" Someone is fighting against our way of life, what we stand for and believe. They are taking away our values, and we must not pick and choose what to follow or not follow in the Bible. We need to take the Bible as is - there are no half-truths.

The straw that will assuredly break the camels' back for the downfall of our country is the incessant and deliberate disobedience to the Word of God in regard to homosexuality. Our rebellion against God was made clear when the US Supreme Court ruled in favor of same sex marriage on July 26, 2015.

The following paragraph is what the Bible says and it is clear enough so any person can understand this.

"22 Thou shalt not lie with mankind, as with womankind: it is abomination.
23 Neither shalt thou lie with any beast to defile thyself therewith: neither shall any woman stand before a beast to lie down thereto: it is confusion.
24 Defile not ye yourselves in any of these things: for in all these the nations are defiled which I cast out before you:

25 And the land is defiled: therefore I do visit the iniquity thereof upon it, and the land itself vomiteth out her inhabitants"

-Leviticus 18:22-25

"21 Because that, when they knew God, they glorified him not as God, neither were thankful; but became vain in their imaginations, and their foolish heart was darkened.

22 Professing themselves to be wise, they became fools,

23 And changed the glory of the uncorruptible God into an image made like to corruptible man, and to birds, and fourfooted beasts, and creeping things.

24 Wherefore God also gave them up to uncleanness through the lusts of their own hearts, to dishonour their own bodies between themselves:

25 Who changed the truth of God into a lie, and worshipped and served the creature more than the Creator, who is blessed for ever. Amen"

- Romans 1:21-25

"Know ye not that the unrighteous shall not inherit the kingdom of God? Be not deceived: neither fornicators, nor idolaters, nor adulterers, nor effeminate, nor abusers of themselves with mankind…"

- Corinthians 6:9

I did not write this; the Pope did not write this; the Evangelical Christians did not write this; but the Almighty God wrote those words. For those of us who believe in the Biblical principles of truth, it is clear that anyone who endorses homosexual lifestyle is not against us, but rather, against the Almighty God. For those of you who lay claim to faith and it's accompanying moral values, from where do you draw your standards? We are intelligent people who can make sound decisions on a daily basis. We have been doing this for a long time. We make decisions as simple as choosing our cell phone plan and as complex as choosing to pursue higher education, a career, to purchase a home, start a business, or to marry. We make these important decisions with a sound mind.

Then how is it when it comes to something that will destroy our way of living and something that will have eternal effects on our soul do we take it so casually? Let us think for a moment, even if someone doesn't agree with my opinion, they know in their hearts that some things are changing and some things are not right, so they should not just let it go. They must do their homework and seek the truth.

To give you a perspective, about seven billion people populate the earth today. Out of that number, an estimated 33 million are refugees. They are running away from what we are forcing ourselves into, the resulting danger, destruction and poverty of a society absent of the Almighty God. So far, even though this is a very large number of the world's population, one does not find any Americans among this group of refugees.

I know this for a fact because I am one of them, and I work with refugees here in the United States and abroad. You may say to me, "We have been ungodly all along." I know this because I realize no one is perfect, but the Founding Fathers started this nation on Godly principles. I've included a transcript of the Declaration of Independence at the close of this book.

God always honors these principles. In the closing words of our Declaration of Independence, the Founding Fathers' supporting pledge was "…with a firm reliance on the protection of divine Providence." That is one of the secrets for the continued blessing from God on this nation. This is not the only secret. Another is found in the Bible, where it is written that any nation that blesses and protects Abram and his descendants, which was to become Israel, God will bless and protect that nation.

"2 And I will make of thee a great nation, and I will bless thee, and make thy name great; and thou shalt be a blessing:
3 And I will bless them that bless thee, and curse him that curseth thee: and in thee shall all families of the earth be blessed"

-Genesis 12:2-3

The United States has a long and rich history of support for the nation of Israel. We have been the beneficiary of relative peace and great prosperity because of this. This nation carries the distinction as a place of refuge for those who suffer religious persecution and other atrocities at the hands of tyrants and dictators from around the world. If we want to continue this "life and blessing" from God we must never shrink back from our support of Israel and others suffering at the hands of the ungodly.

Chapter Five
Foundation

As people of influence, we need to realize that there are certain competencies in our lives that lie dormant until a crisis or a challenge helps us recognize them. Our country was built on certain principles. If we would like to continue enjoying our way of life we need to follow these same principles.

"When in the Course of human events, it becomes necessary for one people to dissolve the political bands which have connected them with another, and to assume among the powers of the earth, the separate and equal station to which the Laws of Nature and of Nature's God entitle them, a decent respect to the opinions of mankind requires that they should declare the causes which impel them to the separation."
- Opening paragraph of "The Unanimous Declaration of the Thirteen United States of America)

Our Founding Fathers knew that blessing and wisdom was rooted in the fear God. Providing justice and liberty were unalienable rights from God and building this nation for the people with this in mind was pleasing to God. For this reason God loves this great nation. He has blessed it tremendously and since we are a blessed nation, our generosity has gone out to the rest of the world.

For the continued blessing and abundance that we've experienced this far, we need to heed the warnings of the great leaders that brought us through the trials of our past.

Without religion the government of a free people cannot be maintained.

"Of all the dispositions and habits which lead to political prosperity, religion and morality are indispensable supports.... And let us with caution indulge the supposition that morality can be maintained without religion"

- George Washington

"I urge you by all that is dear, by all that is honorable, by all that is sacred, not only that ye pray but that ye act"

- John Hancock

"All the armies of Europe, Asia and Africa combined, with all the treasure of the earth (our own excepted) in their military chest; with a Buonaparte for a commander, could not by force, take a drink from the Ohio, or make a track on the Blue Ridge, in a trial of a thousand years"

- Abraham Lincoln, addressing the Young Men's Lyceum of Springfield, Illinois, January 27, 1838

"Today the whole world is divided: divided between human slavery and the human freedom – between pagan brutality and the Christian ideal. We choose human freedom, which is the Christian ideal. No one of us can waver for a moment in his courage or his faith."

- Franklin Delano Roosevelt

"For the invisible things of him from the creation of the world are clearly seen, being understood by the things that are made, even his eternal power and Godhead; so that they are without excuse"
- Romans 1:20

It seems like we are reverting back to what the previous generations warned us of. It's in our best interests to take to heart this wise advice for the securing of our future and that for our children. It's time we come to our senses. But if we turn a deaf ear to our forefather's advice and lose sight of God's Word, disaster will come upon us with no one to blame but ourselves.

"8 Babylon is suddenly fallen and destroyed: howl for her; take balm for her pain, if so be she may be healed.
9 We would have healed Babylon, but she is not healed: forsake her, and let us go every one into his own country: for her judgment reacheth unto heaven, and is lifted up even to the skies.
10 The Lord hath brought forth our righteousness: come, and let us declare in Zion the work of the Lord our God.
11 Make bright the arrows; gather the shields: the Lord hath raised up the spirit of the kings of the Medes: for his device is against Babylon, to destroy it; because it is the vengeance of the Lord, the vengeance of his temple.
12 Set up the standard upon the walls of Babylon, make the watch strong, set up the watchmen, prepare the ambushes: for the Lord hath both devised and done that which he spake

against the inhabitants of Babylon.

¹³ O thou that dwellest upon many waters, abundant in treasures, thine end is come, and the measure of thy covetousness.

¹⁴ The Lord of hosts hath sworn by himself, saying, Surely I will fill thee with men, as with caterpillers; and they shall lift up a shout against thee.

¹⁵ He hath made the earth by his power, he hath established the world by his wisdom, and hath stretched out the heaven by his understanding"

- Jeremiah 51:8-15

I believe this warning is for us today. If it comes to pass, will our society that has lived in such luxury and untold blessing be able to adjust?

When one looks around today so many people are openly mocking the values and virtues that we once cherished in America. But I ask, "Is any one of us able to live a life as we know it without the offerings America once provided?"

It seems that our society today has bought into a big lie and is heading down a perilous road. Many nations that travelled down this same path of rebellion, to include turning from God, learned these lessons and then after much strife turned back to Him. Their repentance is the reason they're doing well today - Bosnia and Ethiopia are just a few examples. God is back in their schools, their military and public places.

On the contrary, let's look at world history and consider powerful nations such as the Roman Empire, the British Empire, or even Hitler's Germany – just to mention a few that have strayed from God. If you trace back to what you thought was the obvious condition that set the stage for the downfall, but then go back a just bit further, it's there where you'll find a more obscure cause for their downfall - the removal of God from society.

Let us save ourselves the heartache and let us turn back to God. Do the right thing for the sake of ourselves. Let us get back doing what we are good at doing, which is creating new innovations, inventing products that advance and better our lives and world -- great things for which only America is known best for doing.

What I know of America is that in this great nation ordinary people take pride in working hard to establish businesses, invent new products, and not settle for anything less than the very best. In American we always strive to achieve new goals and growth.

Even things that are already functioning and working well can be improved. Ongoing improvements of goals and an incredible ability to promote growth. These are some of things that I have observed that America does best. That was possible because America is structured in the way that each of its citizens is given the opportunity to receive fair compensation for hard work, reaping the benefits of their labor.

Unlike many places in the world that only allow a few to benefit from its bounty, the uniqueness of our system allows many people to partake of the many opportunities available; that is one of the best qualities of this nation. That is why our founders and the previous generations fought to set us free from England. They wanted to keep us free so each one of us could reap the fruit of our labor instead of working to enrich the monarchy an unknown king in a far off land.

For those who believe life is just, what happens will happen, why then was the war with England necessary? As we all know that was not the case. Even though we have forgotten the price that was paid to make this nation what it is and in the position it is today, on whose shoulders did we get this far? The previous generations and leaders realized this and foretold of our present situation when they cautioned us. They warned that if we did not continue to obey God and His Word, as is written in the Bible, we would not remain in His prosperity and blessing.

In George Washington's Inaugural Address of 1789 he stated in an almost prophetic way that;

"...we ought to be no less persuaded that the propitious smiles of Heaven, can never be expected on a nation that disregards the eternal rules of order and right, which Heaven itself has ordained."

This is a very important truth for us Americans if our way of life is cherished and worth protecting.

I am not just crying "wolf" for fun. I've had firsthand experience of this in my home country when, following the ousting of Emperor Haile Selassie in 1974, a government that adopted a communist ideology assumed power. This ideology that emphasizes State control of property, business, and most every other aspect of life made no provision for God in its society. I lived through the fallout of this upheaval in the following years. I know how this has affected me personally and the impact it's had on millions of others.

The American Founders understood that no nation will continue in success without God. The key to the success of the early Americans was clearly their adherence to biblical principles. There is no substitute. As we all know our motto, as shown on our currency coins and notes, indicates that our pride is not in our wealth. Even though we are a wealthy nation we chose to "In God We Trust" because our forefathers understood that blessings come from God.

Even President Thomas Jefferson, the man who coined the phrase *"separation of church and state,"* saw a vital need for the worship of God within the very halls of Congress. He signed a law allowing the U.S. Capitol to be used for weekly Christian church services, in which he attended. We have become a nation that openly considers Christianty and God as evil, and we openly practice and celebrate the detestable things.

In recent years we see good and call it evil, and see evil and call it good. It seems as if our personal preferences are shaping our way of life today, instead of allowing absolute truth to be our guiding principles. Let us think for a minute, if we believe in such a thing by what standard are we to judge evil? In reality no one lives that way. If that were true we would need to ask ourselves this very question, "If the standard is just relative, then how is your standard better than any one else's? Where is the supposed evil that religion has caused?" Within a standard based on "personal preference" there is no such thing as good or evil. Let me give you an example: If we say we live with just a personal preference, you have to consider the Nuremberg trials at the close of World War II, in which the Allied forces put numerous officers in the Germany military and leaders in the Nazi Party on trial for war crimes. The argument that the lawyers for the officers and Nazis made was that these men were simply complying with what their culture told them.

That was acceptable to them, therefore, by what standard were the Allied forces using to charge them under? How can these men be tried for the horrendous crimes that their culture supposedly found acceptable? The trial shut down for a few weeks and no one knew how to continue. The prosecuting attorneys for the Allied forces responded by saying that there was a law above the law of man to which they could appeal. Such a law can only exist if God exists, and because if God does exist, there is now a mind superior to the minds of human beings that can define morality. With God it is possible to have a moral absolute because now there is a standard to which all people can be held accountable.

There is not a supreme court, society, or judge who can change what God has set in place. He has the last say whether we like it, or believe it. What God says stands firm and unchanging. God is not made nervous by our decisions and destructive behavior. We are the ones who need to be concerned and mindful of our rebellious ways because they will affect us all - not Him.

Think for a moment if someone assaulted someone, or committed robbery against them, or murdered a loved one, or did all that was terrible to another; could the family or victims honestly say that it was just the perpetrator's personal preference and they would be okay with the crimes committed? No, they would likely seek justice, but by what standard?

In the standard of moral relativism? In that case we are contradicting ourselves. If we do not have a conviction of God's standard to stand on, which by definition is the ultimate truth, then we're just standing on shifting sand. We can confuse and destroy our society by removing the basis for "the rule of law."

There exists a clear distinction between right and wrong and there is a law of God, which is above all other law. If we violate this law we will suffer the consequences. Our present culture is just trying to come up with any idea that goes against the Word of God, but there is no solid truth on the side of such rebellion.

Of course many of us have no idea what the rest of the world looks like. The very reason I am writing this book is because I see so many things that remind me of my past and it scares me for the future of America. Every well-functioning society must have a moral virtue to govern itself. When we diminish that system, we will diminish our way of living. We need to examine every action and decision we make. Just because we are doing things for the first time does not mean it is right.

Chapter Six
Religious Indignation

An effective leader understands that it is often good and wise that we learn from other's mistakes and experiences. This can save them from both distress and sorrow. In my opinion, we are presently heading into unknown territory - unknown to most of us Americans. For many, unexpected struggles and much suffering will accompany this journey. My hope is that people will learn from my story and many others who, like me, are first generation Americans trying to warn this nation.

"My people are destroyed for lack of knowledge"
- Hosea 4:6

I found the classic example of this in an excellent piece written by T. Rees Shapiro in The Washington Post *(March 2012)*. It was about Retired Army Col Van T. Barfoot's struggle with his homeowners association and their laws that prohibited him from flying an American flag in his own front yard.

This American soldier fought in three separate wars for the freedom of others and also for the freedoms we enjoy here in our country. After all the sacrifice from this war hero his right to hoist "old glory" in his own front yard was now being denied by his own countrymen. If they only knew all he had done to secure their rights in the first place. What the homeowner association failed to understand is before you could even have any bylaws for a homeowner's association, you have to have personal property rights to even own a home in this country.

Reading Mr. Barfoot's story draws parallels to what we are trying to do by taking God out of the very nation that God established and blessed. Imagine, trying to take God out is like denying your very identity. The freedom we have and the ways of life itself are God's gifts. Taking God out of this nation is no different from how the homeowner association was trying to stop Mr. Van. T. Barfoot from flying the very flag that he fought to defend all along.

Surely our country is heading in the wrong direction -- no question about it. Some may look around and see the brokenness of our system but you say; "What can I do? I'm just one person." I want to remind us all what the Bible says to do in any given time.

"Finally, brethren, whatsoever things are true, whatsoever things are honest, whatsoever things are just, whatsoever things are pure, whatsoever things are lovely, whatsoever things are of good report; if there be any virtue, and if there be any praise, think on these things"
- Philippians 4:8

That is what God wants us all to do. After reading a story like that of Mr. Barfoot's, one needs to consider where our rights and our way of life come from in the first place. Today's America seems fixed on getting rid of God from our public squares, and our society is doing this in the name of personal rights. But we seem to have forgotten that the rights we enjoy now weren't freely handed to us - there was and still remains a heavy price for us to have this unique freedom. Dismantling our way of life and disregarding the freedoms our Founding Fathers and our previous generations had paid so dearly to obtain would be shameful and reprehensible.

Life gives back what we put into it. We have to be willing to change our bad habits and way of thinking if we want a different outcome. If we want to continue living our lives in America, as we knew it, we need to change our output. Life is like a farm; you only reap what you sow. This ideology that is making its mission to create self-hatred and self-shame for being an American needs to change. That is the language of our enemies. Meanwhile, people all over the world still see America as the land of opportunity. The odd thing about that is many are apologizing for America while enjoying what America has to offer. We cannot have it both ways.

I will remind my readers that there are many millions of people who would love to be in their shoes and they appreciate what America stands for and has to offer. The fact is today's ideology of rebellion against God is like a wildfire. It starts small but as it grows it becomes more difficult to stop. In this country we have everything, and sometimes, more than we need. Yet we complain, murmur, and come off as an ungrateful society.

That is how we can destroy our lives from the inside out. I came to America, this great nation, as a first generation refugee. In a few short years after my arrival I become a homeowner and a business owner. I was able to help my family myself and many others. That was only possible because I was here in America. Nowhere else could someone in my position even dream of such a thing!

In recent years I started sharing my story and bringing awareness about refugees. The doors to this opportunity had opened for me to speak in many colleges, churches and other public venues. My hope is that people can learn from my experience and avoid the difficulties I experienced in my journey. My observation and realization is that many people have no idea what it's like for someone who's become a refugee, or believe such a situation even exists. It is my desire, through speaking, to shed some light on that reality by sharing my story. I want it to be known just how the change came to my home country, and how quickly Ethiopia changed from a kingdom to socialist nation. As a result of this change, I lost my parents at the age of five and became an orphan.

Afraid, alone and searching for a way to save my brothers, I decided to marry at the early age of sixteen. Two of my brothers were then forcibly conscripted into the ensuing war and were later lost. When this strategy proved unsuccessful, I ran away to save my own life and the life of my unborn child. Not knowing where my next meal or shelter might come from, I walked at night and hid during the day to avoid the socialist soldiers and the corrupt police. My goal was to cross the border into Kenya and turn myself in as a refugee.

I was raped three times by the time I reached the refugee camp and was also thrown in jail in a foreign country. What I am sharing is real and it is from my heart. It took me three months to get to the neighboring country. This ordeal was nerve racking, frightening and agonizing for me as a teenager.

"11 If they obey and serve him, they shall spend their days in prosperity, and their years in pleasures.
12 But if they obey not, they shall perish by the sword, and they shall die without knowledge"
-Job 36: 11-12

These verses are not talking about a scholastic degree. They talk about the importance of knowing the truth about God's character and how deeply He cares for His people.

"26 And said, If thou wilt diligently hearken to the voice of the Lord thy God, and wilt do that which is right in his sight, and wilt give ear to his commandments, and keep all his statutes, I will put none of these diseases upon thee, which I have brought upon the Egyptians: for I am the Lord that healeth thee.

²⁷ And they came to Elim, where were twelve wells of water, and threescore and ten palm trees: and they encamped there by the waters"

- Exodus 15:26-27

No doubt God loves America and He has a plan for this great nation. His desire is not to destroy us, but to bless us. On the other hand, as the passage demonstrates, blessings come with conditions and responsibility. The Scriptures I cited above say that at the end they came to Elim. To appreciate this statement, one needs to understand that the children of Israel had been traveling in the desert for a long time. All of a sudden, to arrive where there were twelve springs and seventy palm trees would be like finally reaching paradise. When we have been symbolically traveling through the desert, experiencing a difficult and dry season ourselves, arriving at "Elim," or getting the break and success we have been waiting for, may seem as if we have it all.

However, the children of Israel did not settle in Elim, they continued on to the promised land. From the time of their arrival in their promised land until now, many enemies have raised up to destroy and wipe this tiny nation off the face of the earth. In spite of fierce opposition, they do not just survive, but thrive. After being displaced around the world for thousands of years, they have not only kept their faith and culture, but also their language. That is only possible by the hand of God. Our Founders also realized that God destined this country, for greatness.

That purpose can still be fulfilled as long as we are willing to repent and turn back to Him.

We are still just in "Elim." There is a promised land where bigger and better things are waiting for us if we are willing and obey God and listen to His words. God has given us a manual by which to function as a society. That is the Bible. A good example how this works in real life is made clear if we consider an operator's manual. We all use when we buy new equipment. The manual is the maker's mind or instructions for how to use a given product without any abuse to this specific product.

Imagine driving a vehicle and the maker of that vehicle has provided a manual (the makers mind) on how to operate that vehicle. The vehicle's manual had instructions for the buyer and operator to use unleaded gasoline only. Since the operator likes apple juice he decides to fill the tank with apple juice. Now the vehicle begins malfunctioning. Can one say the manufacturer was unfair?

No, the manufacturer recommends that unleaded gasoline be used because he knows what he is doing. He had tested his product and knows that unleaded is the best option for that vehicle. The vehicle's functions are guaranteed with unleaded gasoline and whatever else the manual says. The operator can protest all he wants, he can even take the manfacturer to court, but nothing will make him change his mind. Why?

Because manufacturer created that vehicle to function with unleaded gasoline only. He may not even say why this is so. One just needs to obey the manual to guarantee the success of the vehicle's function.

The operator can go ahead and change the engine to accommodate the apple juice instead of the unleaded gasoline, but in time the operator will agree it's in his best interest to change his own mind for the success of his vehicle rather than change the mind of the vehicle's maker.

In our daily life we all use manuals to achieve full benefit of the products we purchase. Product disclaimers aways warn us "read and follow directions before use." If we follow and obey the instructions we are most likely guaranteed success.

As long as we are within guidelines of that manual we can enjoy the benefits according to the instructions. The only time we will be on our own with the product we purchased is when we do not follow the manual's instructions and abuse the product. The manual has laws for success. If for some reason, the product does not work when one followed the manual, they have the right to return it. As we all know, here in United States, the manufacture will replace a defective product at no charge. Why do they do that? They do it because their name is on it. They do it to protect their product names.

This isn't done because they know the buyers; it has nothing to do with knowing them. It's all about maintaining a good reputation of their product.

When it comes to our life, there is no difference. We bear God's image. We are His product. That is why our forefathers chose the motto, "In God We Trust." They understood that blessings and wealth come from God. They were showing to whom the image of the product belongs. When we take God's name out of our public squares, our schools, and our Constitution, God is not responsible to protect us anymore. Why? Because we are stripping His label from our country. As we all know, no company protects a product that does not belong to it. If we need to continually have God's protection and blessing the way we used to, then we need to follow the Bible, our "manual." There is no other way.

"26 Behold, I set before you this day a blessing and a curse;
27 A blessing, if ye obey the commandments of the Lord your God, which I command you this day:
28 And a curse, if ye will not obey the commandments of the Lord your God, but turn aside out of the way which I command you this day, to go after other gods, which ye have not known"

- Deuteronomy 11:26-28

"If my people, which are called by my name, shall humble themselves, and pray, and seek my face, and turn from their wicked ways; then will I hear from heaven, and will forgive their sin, and will heal their land"

- Chronicles 7:14

The key words are *"my name."*

Chapter Seven
Misrepresented

It is quite common to meet someone associated with a bad experience they had in church and with Christianity. God has been misrepresented from the very beginning. Let's take a look at the very first misrepresentation of God.

"Now the serpent was more subtil than any beast of the field which the Lord God had made. And he said unto the woman, Yea, hath God said, Ye shall not eat of every tree of the garden"

- Genesis 3:1

Plenty of blame can go around on so-called "Christianity." This may have caused you hurt in the past or you might even be going through a situation right now. I would sincerely like to apologize on God's behalf; He has nothing to do with it - I have been scarred by bad experiences as well. I guarantee you that what God has for His people is never pain, but love. I could tell you this even though we have been misused and mistreated; my people, God is willing and able to heal and restore. He is more than eager to prove to us His love and compassion; I'm the living testament of that. It is an easy way out to rebel and run away when we are hurting but may I suggest that we run to Him instead of from Him because His loving arms are still open to any one of us willing to be embraced and to rest there in.

I am just a simple person who is observing what has been going on in our society today and it saddens my heart for this country. It is a beautiful country. It is such a shame and so sad to see it being destroyed through the act of self-destruction. I believe most of Americans have no idea what it is like to have lived a life without having all the rights we have and all the privileges we enjoy in this country. Most have been living in this country for many generations, and this is all they are familiar with. We think the rest of the world lives just the way we do. Because of that lack of understanding, we have no appreciation for what we have. When we don't appreciate what we have, we place no value on it.

Those changes are taking place slowly and subtly. Without realizing it, we are becoming like the metaphor of a frog in a pot of water that is gradually brought to its boiling point - we are adjusting ourselves to our own death. It's in our best interest to be mindful and to consider this thought, "At least I owe it to myself and to my family to look into this "what if" scenario."

If God lifts His hand from this country, most of us have no idea what will happen to us, and what such a situation could mean. If we become like other nations that rebelled against God, every American needs to ask this very question; "Am I able to handle it?"

Most of us immigrated to this country, or our ancestors did, because we were running away from the same conditions this country is now starting to embrace, what irony. Our home countries have already paid the price for going down the path of rebellion against our Maker. This is the only country in the history of the world where democrats, republicans, independents and even socialist - the entire political group work together peacefully. That's the beauty of this nation, but I'm doubtful if this will be possible in the near future.

In the recent years I was able to go back to the refugee camps and make a difference in the lifes of those who were displaced from their homes. This was only made possible because I live in America and I have the platform and friends who can contribute to my cause. Because I am an American, I have become a spokesperson for many women around the world who are voiceless. I also believe if we destroy our way of living we lose our influential position on the global stage resulting in the destruction of many lives around the world. We may no longer be able to speak on the behalf of those who are vulnerable, those with no one to advocate for their salvation, and those who are weak with no one to defend them. We are already seeing the effects of these changes today.

The challenging issues those situations present to us are real. Our culture today has become so secular, so anti-God. When a society governs itself with moral virtues, it thrives; but when we diminish that system we will diminish our way of living. We've heard statements similar to this coming from various segments of our society,

"We hate what America stands for and has been standing for." I don't understand this position for the life of me, but do they honestly and fully understand what that means? There are many millions of people elsewhere in the world willing to trade places with them. Do they realize that the poorest person in our nation is far better off than most other places in the world? I could honestly testify to the fact that there is no place in the world like the United States of America. I don't think we realize how blessed we are!

Do not just take my words for it. While campaigning for Presidential candidate Barry Goldwater, the late Ronald Reagan spoke of the maintenance of peace as being what the opposition party believed to be the main issue in the upcoming election. Here's an excerpt from Reagan's October 27, 1964, *"A Time for Choosing"* speech:

"As for the peace that we would preserve, I wonder who among us would like to approach the wife or mother whose husband or son has died in South Vietnam and ask them if they think this is a peace that should be maintained indefinitely. Do they mean peace, or do they mean we just want to be left in peace? There can be no real peace while one American is dying some place in the world for the rest of us. We're at war with the most dangerous enemy that has ever faced mankind in his long climb from the swamp to the stars, and it's been said if we lose that war, and in so doing lose this way of free-

dom of ours, history will record with the greatest astonishment that those who had the most to lose did the least to prevent its happening. Well I think it's time we ask ourselves if we still know the freedoms that were intended for us by the Founding Fathers. Not too long ago, two friends of mine were talking to a Cuban refugee, a businessman who had escaped from Castro, and in the midst of his story one of my friends turned to the other and said, "We don't know how lucky we are." And the Cuban stopped and said, "How lucky you are? I had someplace to escape to." And in that sentence he told us the entire story. If we lose freedom here, there's no place to escape to. This is the last stand on earth."

Ronald Reagan went on to say;

"And this idea that government is beholden to the people, that it has no other source of power except the sovereign people, is still the newest and the most unique idea in all the long history of man's relation to man. This is the issue of this election: Whether we believe in our capacity for self-government or whether we abandon the American revolution and confess that a little intellectual elite in a far-distant capitol can plan our lives for us better than we can plan them ourselves."

We will regret that we didn't accept and follow God when we had the opportunity. There is no substitute for full understanding of what this means and it's been hard for people to understand the reason many of us came to be refugees. I have been repeatedly asked why so many people were displaced and became refugees in the first place. Of course my answer usually includes the fact that someone else's choice of ideology dictated the outcome of my life and the result was me becoming a refugee. Unfortunately, I was born in a country and during a time when only those in power had the voice and the guns.

Chapter Eight
Not My Choice

Many of the people in the world today are in similar situations; they don't have a voice when it comes to making a choice for their lives. Most of them have nothing to do with the outcome of their lives and someone else is creating the conditions of their lives. We live in a country where our voice means something, and every individual can change things and make a difference in a small or larger scale regardless of age, gender, skin color, class or background. I worry that we are about to lose that very right. If we keep turning away from the fundamental ideas of the Founding Fathers we may find ourselves living like most other people in the world. That is not something we should take lightly.

I share this from my heart after years of struggle. Many have been scattered all over the world as refugees and many millions have lost their lives. Today it is like water under a bridge for many Ethiopians, but at the time you couldn't find a single person that hadn't been affected by the changes that took place in my country.

The courage it took for me to leave my homeland with nothing more than the cloths on my back and a baby in my womb was unquestionably the grace of God. When I was caught and thrown in jail for three weeks with only the concrete floor to sleep on, I know that the very hands of God became my mattress, sheet, blanket and pillow. He is still with me. He gave me the grace and the courage to walk through those dark nights while being so frightened, scared and lonely.

There was a time I was without any hope. I often found myself not knowing which direction I was heading, and with little certainty of when, or if, I would reach my destination.

His hand was with me when I reached the refugee camp in Kenya, and when it was time for me to give birth to my first child as a teen mom. He was with me when during the delivery as two of us women were experiencing labor on a twin-sized bed and afterward through the C-section with four of us on that same bed.

I do not know about anyone else, but my survival in the face of such trials could only come from God. I am certain that for the last thirty plus years the same hand has been guiding and sustaining me. I am well aware of the existence of God, He is not fiction nor mythical - He is real and I do talk to Him every single day.

For all of us mankind, faith is a compass that guides us and defines our core values. When we lose direction, how are we to govern others or ourselves? How do we know right from wrong if we have no faith in God or fear in Him? Here's an example where two midwives, Shiphrah and Puah, disobeyed Pharaoh, king of Egypt, because of their fear of the Lord.

"*15 And the king of Egypt spake to the Hebrew midwives, of which the name of the one was Shiphrah, and the name of the other Puah:*

16 And he said, When ye do the office of a midwife to the Hebrew women, and see them upon the stools; if it be a son, then ye shall kill him: but if it be a daughter, then she shall live.
17 But the midwives feared God, and did not as the king of Egypt commanded them, but saved the men children alive"

- Exodus 1:15-17

That is the moral compass and the value of faith. There's a lesson to be learned from Ethiopia and their attempt to rid itself of Christianity. God did not vanish like they hoped, but the people did- God is still on His throne. It is necessary to say that God does not need us; it is us who need Him so desperately. I'm sure if, not now, a day will surely come when we as a nation will realize this truth. It is wise to trust and obey Him. Will you take this opportunity?

" Jesus Christ the same yesterday, and to day, and for ever"

- Hebrews 13:8

We may say we have everything we need and that we have no need for God. This is what the Word of God says about the people who hold such a view.

"16 So then because thou art lukewarm, and neither cold nor hot, I will spue thee out of my mouth.
17 Because thou sayest, I am rich, and increased with goods, and have need of nothing; and

106

knowest not that thou art wretched, and miserable, and poor, and blind, and naked:

[18] I counsel thee to buy of me gold tried in the fire, that thou mayest be rich; and white raiment, that thou mayest be clothed, and that the shame of thy nakedness do not appear; and anoint thine eyes with eyesalve, that thou mayest see.

[19] As many as I love, I rebuke and chasten: be zealous therefore, and repent.

[20] Behold, I stand at the door, and knock: if any man hear my voice, and open the door, I will come in to him, and will sup with him, and he with me.

[21] To him that overcometh will I grant to sit with me in my throne, even as I also overcame, and am set down with my Father in his throne.

[22] He that hath an ear, let him hear what the Spirit saith unto the churches"

- Revelation 3:16-22

Life without God is like a captain trying to steer a ship on open sea without a compass, or much like trying to operate machinery or any equipment without a manual. It is very difficult. Remember, no company protects a product that doesn't belong to them.

"And God said, Let us make man in our image, after our likeness: and let them have dominion over the fish of the sea, and over the fowl of the air, and over the cattle, and over all the earth, and over every creeping thing that creepeth upon the earth"

- Genesis 1:26

God is not responsible to protect us because we are stripping his label from our identity, our constitution. By doing so, we are responsible for losing God's protection.

"If my people, which are called by my name, shall humble themselves, and pray, and seek my face, and turn from their wicked ways; then will I hear from heaven, and will forgive their sin, and will heal their land"

-Chronicles 7:14

Again, we must remember that the key word in this verse is "my name." God reveals to redeem! In the book of Deuteronomy God gives us a choice between life and its blessings or death and its destruction and then suggests we choose life. If we turn our hearts back to God, He has promised in his Word to heal us. There is always a second chance with God, if we are willing!

We read in the Bible a story about a man named Nehemiah who was so sorrowful because he got the bad news about his country and his people:

"1 The words of Nehemiah the son of Hachaliah. And it came to pass in the month Chisleu, in the twentieth year, as I was in Shushan the palace,
2 That Hanani, one of my brethren, came, he and certain men of Judah; and I asked them concerning the Jews that had escaped, which were left of the captivity, and concerning Jerusalem.

³ And they said unto me, The remnant that are left of the captivity there in the province are in great affliction and reproach: the wall of Jerusalem also is broken down, and the gates thereof are burned with fire.
⁴ And it came to pass, when I heard these words, that I sat down and wept, and mourned certain days, and fasted, and prayed before the God of heaven" (Nehemiah 1:1-4).

Nehemiah said, "When I heard these things, I sat down" That means when he got the news it was so sad he could not go on with business as usual. So, he cleared his calendar, sat down and quieted himself. Why? Because if we just continue on our treadmill, we will never have an opportunity to meditate and see what is going wrong.

Today we are witnessing our great nation's foundation being broken. We need to sit, weep and mourn. We cannot go on as if everything is okay. When we sit down and quiet ourselves, then we will have passion and an opportunity to realize the messy situation in which we are currently living. Then we can say, "Wait a minute. What have we come into?" We can ask ourselves, "So now what can I do to rebuild this great nation?"

Only when we give ourselves time to quiet down, can we begin to have a vision of what needs to be done, to come to a realization of what our past looked like when our walls were standing strong and our gates were still secure - symbolically speaking.

We have left to good path that was intended for this nation – the good life spoken of by our earlier generations. Let us stop demonizing America and let us reflect on where we went wrong so that we can come together and rebuild our country. Let us again make God the center of our lives and our nation. God is not done with us yet! In my opinion God has planned even bigger and better things yet to come for this nation. We haven't arrived at our destination yet. We can go higher as long as we are willing to walk hand in hand with God.

Appendix

I close with an excerpt from President George Washington's Farewell Address, 1796. It is clear to see that George Washington cherished and understood the "immense value" of this new nation, and undoubtedly, what some twenty years earlier encouraged his "appeal to heaven."

"...The unity of government which constitutes you one people is also now dear to you. It is justly so, for it is a main pillar in the edifice of your real independence, the support of your tranquility at home, your peace abroad; of your safety; of your prosperity; of that very liberty which you so highly prize.

But as it is easy to foresee that, from different causes and from different quarters, much pains will be taken, many artifices employed to weaken in your minds the conviction of this truth; as this is the point in your political fortress against which the batteries of internal and external enemies will be most constantly and actively (though often covertly and insidiously) directed, it is of infinite moment that you should properly estimate the immense value of your national union to your collective and individual happiness;

(T)hat you should cherish a cordial, habitual, and immovable attachment to it; accustoming yourselves to think and speak of it as of the palladium of your political safety and prosperity; watching for its preservation with jealous anxiety; discountenancing whatever may suggest even a suspicion that it can in any event be abandoned; and indignantly frowning upon the first dawning of every attempt to alienate any portion of our country from the rest, or to enfeeble the sacred ties which now link together the various parts..."

Recollection of Patrick Henry's speech addressing the President of the Second Virginia Convention, Peyton Randolph, at St. John's Church, Richmond, Virginia, March 23, 1775

MR. PRESIDENT: No man thinks more highly than I do of the patriotism, as well as abilities, of the very worthy gentlemen who have just addressed the House. But different men often see the same subject in different lights; and, therefore, I hope it will not be thought disrespectful to those gentlemen if, entertaining as I do, opinions of a character very opposite to theirs, I shall speak forth my sentiments freely, and without reserve. This is no time for ceremony. The question before the House is one of awful moment to this country. For my own part, I consider it as nothing less than a question of freedom or slavery; and in proportion to the magnitude of the subject ought to be the freedom of the debate. It is only in this way that we can hope to arrive at truth, and fulfil the great responsibility which we hold to God and our country. Should I keep back my opinions at such a time, through fear of giving offence, I should consider myself as guilty of treason towards my country, and of an act of disloyalty toward the majesty of heaven, which I revere above all earthly kings.

Mr. President, it is natural to man to indulge in the illusions of hope. We are apt to shut our eyes against a painful truth, and listen to the song of that siren till she transforms us into beasts. Is this the part of wise men, engaged in a great and arduous struggle for liberty? Are we disposed to be of the number of those who, having eyes, see not, and, having ears, hear not, the things which so nearly concern their temporal salvation? For my part, whatever anguish of spirit it may cost, I am willing to know the whole truth; to know the worst, and to provide for it.

I have but one lamp by which my feet are guided; and that is the lamp of experience. I know of no way of judging of the future but by the past. And judging by the past, I wish to know what there has been in the conduct of the British ministry for the last ten years, to justify those hopes with which gentlemen have been pleased to solace themselves, and the House? Is it that insidious smile with which our petition has been lately received? Trust it not, sir; it will prove a snare to your feet. Suffer not yourselves to be betrayed with a kiss.

Ask yourselves how this gracious reception of our petition comports with these war-like preparations which cover our waters and darken our land. Are fleets and armies necessary to a work of love and reconciliation? Have we shown ourselves so unwilling to be reconciled, that force must be called in to win back our love? Let us not deceive ourselves, sir. These are the implements of war and subjugation; the last arguments to which kings resort.

I ask, gentlemen, sir, what means this martial array, if its purpose be not to force us to submission? Can gentlemen assign any other possible motive for it? Has Great Britain any enemy, in this quarter of the world, to call for all this accumulation of navies and armies? No, sir, she has none. They are meant for us; they can be meant for no other. They are sent over to bind and rivet upon us those chains which the British ministry have been so long forging. And what have we to oppose to them? Shall we try argument? Sir, we have been trying that for the last ten years. Have we anything new to offer upon the subject? Nothing. We have held the subject up in every light of which it is capable; but it has been all in vain. Shall we resort to entreaty and humble supplication? What terms shall we find which have not been already exhausted?

Let us not, I beseech you, sir, deceive ourselves. Sir, we have done everything that could be done, to avert the storm which is now coming on. We have petitioned; we have remonstrated; we have supplicated; we have prostrated ourselves before the throne, and have implored its interposition to arrest the tyrannical hands of the ministry and Parliament. Our petitions have been slighted; our remonstrances have produced additional violence and insult; our supplications have been disregarded; and we have been spurned, with contempt, from the foot of the throne. In vain, after these things, may we indulge the fond hope of peace and reconciliation. There is no longer any room for hope. If we wish to be free if we mean to preserve inviolate those inestimable privileges for which we have been so long contending if we mean not basely to abandon the noble struggle in which we have been so long engaged, and which we have pledged ourselves never to abandon until the glorious object of our contest shall be obtained, we must fight! I repeat it, sir, we must fight! An appeal to arms and to the God of Hosts is all that is left us!

They tell us, sir, that we are weak; unable to cope with so formidable an adversary. But when shall we be stronger? Will it be the next week, or the next year? Will it be when we are totally disarmed, and when a British guard shall be stationed in every house? Shall we gather strength by irresolution and inaction? Shall we acquire the means of effectual resistance, by lying supinely on our backs, and hugging the delusive phantom of hope, until our enemies shall have bound us hand and foot?

Sir, we are not weak if we make a proper use of those means which the God of nature hath placed in our power. Three millions of people, armed in the holy cause of liberty, and in such a country as that which we possess, are invincible by any force which our enemy can send against us. Besides, sir, we shall not fight our battles alone. There is a just God who presides over the destinies of nations; and who will raise up friends to fight our battles for us. The battle, sir, is not to the strong alone; it is to the vigilant, the active, the brave. Besides, sir, we have no election. If we were base enough to desire it, it is now too late to retire from the contest. There is no retreat but in submission and slavery! Our chains are forged! Their clanking may be heard on the plains of Boston! The war is inevitable and let it come! I repeat it, sir, let it come.

It is in vain, sir, to extenuate the matter. Gentlemen may cry, Peace, Peace but there is no peace. The war is actually begun! The next gale that sweeps from the north will bring to our ears the clash of resounding arms! Our brethren are already in the field! Why stand we here idle? What is it that gentlemen wish? What would they have? Is life so dear, or peace so sweet, as to be purchased at the price of chains and slavery? Forbid it, Almighty God! I know not what course others may take; but as for me, give me liberty or give me death!

IN CONGRESS, July 4, 1776.
The unanimous Declaration of the thirteen united States of America:

When in the Course of human events, it becomes necessary for one people to dissolve the political bands which have connected them with another, and to assume among the powers of the earth, the separate and equal station to which the Laws of Nature and of Nature's God entitle them, a decent respect to the opinions of mankind requires that they should declare the causes which impel them to the separation.

We hold these truths to be self-evident, that all men are created equal, that they are endowed by their Creator with certain unalienable Rights, that among these are Life, Liberty and the pursuit of Happiness.--That to secure these rights, Governments are instituted among Men, deriving their just powers from the consent of the governed, --That whenever any Form of Government becomes destructive of these ends, it is the Right of the People to alter or to abolish it, and to institute new Government, laying its foundation on such principles and organizing its powers in such form, as to them shall seem most likely to effect their Safety and Happiness. Prudence, indeed, will dictate that Governments long established should not be changed for light and transient causes; and accordingly all experience hath shewn, that mankind are more disposed to suffer, while evils are sufferable, than to right themselves by abolishing the forms to which they are accustomed. But when a long train of abuses and usurpations, pursuing invariably the same Object evinces a design to reduce them under absolute Despotism, it is their right, it is their duty, to throw off such Government, and to provide new Guards for their future security.--Such has been the patient sufferance of these Colonies; and such is now the necessity which constrains them to alter their former Systems of Government. The history of the present King of Great Britain is a history of repeated injuries and usurpations, all having in direct object the establishment of an absolute Tyranny over these States. To prove this, let Facts be submitted to a candid world.

He has refused his Assent to Laws, the most wholesome and necessary for the public good.

He has forbidden his Governors to pass Laws of immediate and pressing importance, unless suspended in their operation till his Assent should be obtained; and when so suspended, he has utterly neglected to attend to them.

He has refused to pass other Laws for the accommodation of large districts of people, unless those people would relinquish the right of Representation in the Legislature, a right inestimable to them and formidable to tyrants only.

He has called together legislative bodies at places unusual, uncomfortable, and distant from the depository of their public Records, for the sole purpose of fatiguing them into compliance with his measures.

He has dissolved Representative Houses repeatedly, for opposing with manly firmness his invasions on the rights of the people.

He has refused for a long time, after such dissolutions, to cause others to be elected; whereby the Legislative powers, incapable of Annihilation, have returned to the People at large for their exercise; the State remaining in the mean time exposed to all the dangers of invasion from without, and convulsions within.

He has endeavoured to prevent the population of these States; for that purpose obstructing the Laws for Naturalization of Foreigners; refusing to pass others to encourage their migrations hither, and raising the conditions of new Appropriations of Lands.

He has obstructed the Administration of Justice, by refusing his Assent to Laws for establishing Judiciary powers.

He has made Judges dependent on his Will alone, for the tenure of their offices, and the amount and payment of their salaries.

He has erected a multitude of New Offices, and sent hither swarms of Officers to harrass our people, and eat out their substance.

He has kept among us, in times of peace, Standing Armies without the Consent of our legislatures.

He has affected to render the Military independent of and superior to the Civil power.

He has combined with others to subject us to a jurisdiction foreign to our constitution, and unacknowledged by our laws; giving his Assent to their Acts of pretended Legislation:

For Quartering large bodies of armed troops among us:

For protecting them, by a mock Trial, from punishment for any Murders which they should commit on the Inhabitants of these States:

For cutting off our Trade with all parts of the world:

For imposing Taxes on us without our Consent:

For depriving us in many cases, of the benefits of Trial by Jury:

For transporting us beyond Seas to be tried for pretended offences

For abolishing the free System of English Laws in a neighbouring Province, establishing therein an Arbitrary government, and enlarging its Boundaries so as to render it at once an example and fit instrument for introducing the same absolute rule into these Colonies:

For taking away our Charters, abolishing our most valuable Laws, and altering fundamentally the Forms of our Governments:

For suspending our own Legislatures, and declaring themselves invested with power to legislate for us in all cases whatsoever.

He has abdicated Government here, by declaring us out of his Protection and waging War against us.

He has plundered our seas, ravaged our Coasts, burnt our towns, and destroyed the lives of our people.

He is at this time transporting large Armies of foreign Mercenaries to compleat the works of death, desolation and tyranny, already begun with circumstances of Cruelty & perfidy scarcely paralleled in the most barbarous ages, and totally unworthy the Head of a civilized nation.

He has constrained our fellow Citizens taken Captive on the high Seas to bear Arms against their Country, to become the executioners of their friends and Brethren, or to fall themselves by their Hands.

He has excited domestic insurrections amongst us, and has endeavoured to bring on the inhabitants of our frontiers, the merciless Indian Savages, whose known rule of warfare, is an undistinguished destruction of all ages, sexes and conditions.

In every stage of these Oppressions We have Petitioned for Redress in the most humble terms: Our repeated Petitions have been answered only by repeated injury. A Prince whose character is thus marked by every act which may define a Tyrant, is unfit to be the ruler of a free people.

Nor have We been wanting in attentions to our Brittish brethren. We have warned them from time to time of attempts by their legislature to extend an unwarrantable jurisdiction over us. We have reminded them of the circumstances of our emigration and settlement here. We have appealed to their native justice and magnanimity, and we have conjured them by the ties of our common kindred to disavow these usurpations, which, would inevitably interrupt our connections and correspondence. They too have been deaf to the voice of justice and of consanguinity. We must, therefore, acquiesce in the necessity, which denounces our Separation, and hold them, as we hold the rest of mankind, Enemies in War, in Peace Friends.

We, therefore, the Representatives of the united States of America, in General Congress, Assembled, appealing to the Supreme Judge of the world for the rectitude of our intentions, do, in the Name, and by Authority of the good

People of these Colonies, solemnly publish and declare, That these United Colonies are, and of Right ought to be Free and Independent States; that they are Absolved from all Allegiance to the British Crown, and that all political connection between them and the State of Great Britain, is and ought to be totally dissolved; and that as Free and Independent States, they have full Power to levy War, conclude Peace, contract Alliances, establish Commerce, and to do all other Acts and Things which Independent States may of right do. And for the support of this Declaration, with a firm reliance on the protection of divine Providence, we mutually pledge to each other our Lives, our Fortunes and our sacred Honor.

About the Author

Shegitu Kebede has known first hand what war and refugee camps are like. After fleeing her war torn county of Ethiopia she lived and had her first child in a refugee camp in Kenya and then resettled and gained citizenship in the United States. As the founder of "Going Home" and "Women at the Well International" Shegitu and her husband, along with her children, are committed to enriching the lives of refugees and communities here in the United States and also abroad.

Her work has earned her numerous awards which include; The Virginia Mc'Knight 'Binger Award in Human Services, national recognition from Bridging Refugee Youth and Children's Services, Washington, D.C., featured in a Minnesota History Center exhibit, "The Value of One Life", the Emerald Service Award from the Minneapolis-St. Paul Chapter of The Links Incorporated, a Service Above Self Award from the Minneapolis Chapter of Rotary International, and named a Paul Harris Fellow from The Rotary Foundation of Rotary International.

Shegitu calls Minnesota her home and is a wife, a mother, published author, motivational speaker and volunteer.

Other books by Shegitu
My African Heritage
My American Heritage
Visible Strengths, Hidden Scars

Acknowledgements

First and foremost, I would like to thank my Creator, my Heavenly Father for this opportunity.

I also want to take a moment to thank my earthly friends who have left a permanent mark on my life and in my work. I find it necessary to call you out by name for all the support you've shown me throughout my years, particularly, the difficult ones. Each one of you came into my life at a different time but you all played a crucial role; you've always been someone I could call on. What means the most to me is that you do more for me than I could tell you - thank you!!! Some of you created opportunity or supported the opportunities that came my way. It seems like you remember my achievements even better than I do myself. I always appreciate your ability to see how my gift from God can make a difference and you've made me a stronger believer as well! After a chat with any one of you I always feel more capable and confident, and for that I will always be grateful.

Ann and Carroll Rock, Suzanne Kochevar, Joe Selvaggio, Dr. Hugh Westgate, Mona Carloni, Jane Graupman, Joe Roslansky, Rebecca Booker, Dr. Erica Diehn, Paul Fate, Barbara Jeanetta, Mihailo Temali, Carol Williams, Lynda Shaheen, Anketse Berhanu, Hannah Mariam Dereje, Debrework Damte, Lulsegged Abebe, Fre Haile, Dr. Shamilla Amulega,

Marilyn Matheny, Dorothy Mayer, Carol and Dennis Grina, Ron and Vicki Pollard, Terri Kangas.

There are also many other special people I want to thank but cannot name you all. You have impacted my life in one-way or another. Some people come and go in our lives like passing ships, never meant to be part of our lives, but they are kindred spirits who come into our world and touch our hearts and make a difference in our lives. They give us the gift of friendship so that we are not alone. Friends share simple and ordinary times in our lives, moments that become memories locked in our hearts. I'm so grateful to God for allowing me to be a part of your lives.

Thank you all,
Shegitu